Lives
of the Artists

BOTTICELLI

Lives of the Artists

BOTTICELLI

WORLD ALMANAC® LIBRARY

Please visit our web site at:
www.worldalmanaclibrary.com
For a free color catalog describing World Almanac®
Library's list of high-quality books and multimedia
programs, call 1-800-848-2928 (USA) or 1-800-387-3178
(Canada). World Almanac® Library's fax: (414) 332-3567.

Library of Congress Cataloging-in-Publication Data

Connolly, Sean, 1956-
    Botticelli / by Sean Connolly.
       p. cm. — (Lives of the artists)
    Includes index.
    ISBN 0-8368-5648-1 (lib. bdg.)
    ISBN 0-8368-5653-8 (softcover)
    1. Botticelli, Sandro, 1444 or 5-1510—Juvenile literature.
    2. Painters—Italy—Biography—Juvenile literature. I. Title.
    II. Series.
    ND623.B7C65   2004
    759.5—dc22   2004041295

This North American edition first published in 2005 by
World Almanac® Library
330 West Olive Street, Suite 100
Milwaukee, WI 53212 USA

The series "The Lives of the Artists"
was created and produced by McRae Books Srl
Borgo Santa Croce, 8 – Florence (Italy)
info@mcraebooks.com
Publishers: Anne McRae and Marco Nardi

Project Editor: Loredana Agosta
Art History consultant: Roberto Carvalho de Magalhães
Text: Sean Connolly
Illustrations: Studio Stalio (Alessandro Cantucci,
Fabiano Fabbrucci, Andrea Morandi)
Graphic Design: Marco Nardi
Picture Research: Loredana Agosta
Layout: Studio Yotto

World Almanac® Library editor: JoAnn Early Macken
World Almanac® Library art direction: Tammy Gruenewald

Acknowledgments
All efforts have been made to obtain and provide compensation for
the copyright to the photographs and artworks in this book in accor-
dance with legal provisions. Persons who may nevertheless still have
claims are requested to contact the copyright owners.

t=top; tl=top left; tc=top center; tr=top right; c=center; cl=center
left; cr= center right; b=bottom; bl=bottom left; bc=bottom center;
br=bottom right

The publishers would like to thank the following museums and
archives who have authorized the reproduction of the works in this
book:
The Bridgeman Art Library, London / Farabola Foto, Milano: 10tr,
30–31, 33b, 36tr, 36c, 37, 39br, 41, 42–43, 45t, 45c; Corbis / Contrasto,
Milano: 14cl, 43t; Foto Scala, Florence: cover, 6c, 7tr, 7br, 9tl, 9tr, 9br,
10bl, 11tr, 12bl, 13bl, 13cr, 14cr, 15t, 17tr, 17b, 18cl, 18bl, 19tr, 19tl, 19bl,
19c, 20bl, 21t, 21b, 22tr, 22b, 24r, 25tl, 25br, 26–27, 28–29, 29tl, 29tr, 30tr,
32b, 34b, 35tl, 35b, 38b, 40b, 44c; Staatliche Museen zu Berlin –
Kupferstichkabinett, 23t

Printed in Malaysia

2 3 4 5 6 7 8 9 08

cover: *Primavera* (detail), Uffizi, Florence

opposite: *Primavera* (detail), Uffizi, Florence

previous page: *Portrait of a Man Holding a Medallion of Cosimo de'*
Medici, Uffizi, Florence

Table of Contents

Introduction

Sandro Botticelli (1445–1510), whose religious and allegorical paintings are some of the most famous images in the history of European art, was a master of the Renaissance. Like so many other Renaissance geniuses (notably Leonardo da Vinci and Michelangelo Buonarroti), Botticelli emerged from the Florentine school. Unlike these other artists, however, he worked almost exclusively in Florence, apart from a brief papal commission in the Sistine Chapel. Seemingly overtaken by artistic developments by the end of his life, Botticelli became a prime influence for several art movements in the nineteenth century.

Botticelli's ITALY

Prato
Florence
Rome

▲ *A carved lion by the Florentine sculptor Donatello (1386–1466). The sitting lion, called a* marzocco, *was a symbol of Botticelli's home city, Florence.*

A Master Draftsman

Botticelli was less concerned with linear perspective and other Renaissance artistic "breakthroughs." Instead, he used his natural talent as a draftsman to shine through his works. He was more concerned with the representation of movement, with sinuous, vibrant lines, which make his figures and compositions graceful and flowing. By coupling grace of line with a palette of pale, cool colors, Botticelli was able to create a mysterious, evocative, or even exhilarating effect.

◀ Angel of the Annunciation *(c. 1483–90). Botticelli's drawings reflect the graceful lines of his paintings.*

Beautiful Madonnas

Renaissance Florence in the fifteenth century was a flourishing society that found itself at the forefront of European humanism. Scholars, writers, artists, and patrons celebrated the human spirit and the victory of intellect over base instincts. At the same time, the Christian tradition remained strong, with churches and religious institutions tapping into the exciting new techniques in architecture, sculpture, and painting. Much of Botticelli's output was within this tradition, and in particular, he excelled in his depictions of the Madonna. Some of these paintings were commissioned as private devotional works for wealthy patrons. Others had a more public purpose, serving as altarpieces in the churches and chapels around Florence (see pages 34–35).

▶ *Madonna of the Magnificat (1483–5). Botticelli probably produced the painting for a private client who could have afforded the costly gold paint.*

Great Patrons

Botticelli's Florence was a republic in name. In effect, however, the wealthy Medici family ruled the flourishing city. Medici political supremacy began with Giovanni de' Medici (1360–1429). Giovanni's son, Cosimo the Elder (1389–1464) made himself sole ruler and held power throughout Botticelli's youth. His son Piero (see page 11) and grandson Lorenzo the Magnificent (see page 15) became great patrons of Botticelli.

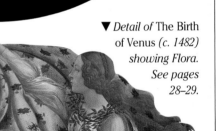

▼ *Detail of* The Birth of Venus *(c. 1482) showing Flora. See pages 28–29.*

Subjects from Classical Mythology

Many of Botticelli's most famous works were allegorical paintings featuring characters and episodes from the classical period. Renaissance scholars rediscovered many of these original stories (just as artists discovered recovered statues). Many of Botticelli's patrons were influenced by Neoplatonism. The Florentine scholars Marsilio Ficino (1433–99) and Angelo Poliziano (1454–94) translated many of Plato's works and tried to meld classical ideals with humanist ideas of Christian piety.

▲ *Opening page of a Marsilio Ficino book dedicated to Lorenzo the Magnificent.*

▶ *Portrait of Cosimo the Elder (1518–20) by Jacopo Pontormo (1494–1557).*

Early Years

Sandro Botticelli was the son of the tanner Mariano di Vanni. Fifteenth-century Florence was leading Europe into the Renaissance. Unlike the situation in other European cities at the time, working-class Florentines such as Mariano had a say in the workings of the city's government. The backbone of Florentine life was a complicated network of guilds. As a tanner, Botticelli's father was a member of one of the Arti Minori (lesser guilds). Members of such guilds, as well as those belonging to the Arti Maggiori (greater guilds), could vote for representatives in the city's two great ruling councils.

▲ *This fifteenth-century Sienese altarpiece, decorated with gold and precious stones, depicts the* Pietà *(Mary mourning the death of Christ).*

▲ *This detail from a mid-fourteenth-century Florentine manuscript shows a leather worker engaged at his trade.*

"Little Barrel"

Botticelli was born Alessandro di Mariano di Vanni Filipepi. "Sandro" is a common Italian diminutive of Alessandro. Botticelli, meaning "Little Barrel," was a nickname given to Sandro's eldest (and stout) brother Giovanni. The name stuck not just to Giovanni and Sandro, but to the other members of the family. However, it hardly fit Sandro, who was a frail and introspective boy.

Renaissance Goldsmiths

Sandro, like his brother Antonio, became an apprentice goldsmith. The distinction between crafts and fine art was less rigid at the time. Artists often trained as goldsmiths, and many prized works of art, such as the glazed colored plaques of the Della Robbia family, were executed by artist–craftsmen.

▶ *Palazzo Rucellai, designed by Leon Battista Alberti (1404–72), is one of the first examples of Florentine Renaissance architecture.*

Prosperous Neighbors

Although Botticelli's family could be described as being working class, they had prosperous and influential neighbors. The Vespucci family (see page 18) later became Sandro's patrons. Some documents indicate that Sandro and his family lived in a house owned by the Rucellai, one of the most influential families in republican Florence.

▼ *Donatello's relief sculpture on a pulpit of San Lorenzo church (c. 1465) presented a grim but beautiful depiction of episodes from the Passion of Christ.*

▲ The Annunciation *(1436–47) was one of about fifty frescoes painted by Fra Angelico and his assistants in the monastery of San Marco in central Florence.*

Masters of the Day

At the time of Botticelli's childhood, mid-fifteenth-century Florence was a hotbed of artistic ideas and mastery. Painters, sculptors, and architects explored new or rediscovered principles of balance, proportion, and harmony. Painters such as Masaccio (1401–28) and Fra Angelico (c. 1400–55) had already presented religious scenes with a new freshness and depth. By the 1450s, Donatello (1386–1466), also based in Florence, was recognized as Europe's leading sculptor. Also by this time, the Cathedral dome, testament to the architectural genius of Filippo Brunelleschi (1377–1446), dominated the city skyline.

Apprenticeship in Prato

Perhaps influenced by the careers of painters who had begun as goldsmiths, Botticelli persuaded his father to let him change professions. When he was sixteen, Sandro became apprenticed to Fra Filippo Lippi (c. 1406–69), a Carmelite monk living in the town of Prato, about 12 miles (20 km) from Florence. Botticelli was a late starter — most apprentices began by age twelve — but Lippi was an excellent teacher, instructing apprentices in the techniques of composition, production, and preparation of paints. Soon Botticelli was contributing backgrounds to Lippi's work, and within about three years, he was painting works of his own.

▶ Madonna and Child with Two Angels *(c. 1465) by Fra Filippo Lippi was typical of the tender devotional style that inspired Botticelli.*

1467 After the departure of Fra Filippo Lippi for Spoleto, Botticelli returns to Florence and continues his apprenticeship at the workshop of Andrea del Verrocchio.

1467–70 At Verrocchio's workshop, Botticelli comes into contact with other young and promising artists, including Leonardo da Vinci. By the end of this decade, he likely attracts the attention of Piero de' Medici and secures his first public commission, from the merchants' guild, for a panel representing the virtue Fortitude.

▼ *Botticelli's debt to Lippi's style is apparent in the intricate treatment of the rich fabrics in his early work* Madonna and Child, Two Angels and the Young Saint John the Baptist *(c. 1468).*

A Fruitful Apprenticeship

▼ *Botticelli's halos were delicate and almost transparent, as seen in this detail from his* Madonna and Child with the Young Saint John the Baptist *(c. 1470).*

From about 1465, Botticelli had moved from providing backgrounds and secondary figures in Lippi's paintings to completing paintings of his own. With this grounding and practical experience, Botticelli was prepared to return to Florence as an artist in his own right when Lippi left Prato for Spoleto in 1467. In Florence, Botticelli was to meet and share ideas with other artists at the workshop of Andrea del Verrocchio.

Golden Halos

The earliest examples of painting golden halos over the heads of holy people are the sun disks in early Persian and ancient Greek works. Medieval Christian artists mixed gold leaf into the paint to signal the special qualities of the saints being painted. The halo itself, however, was usually no more than a flat golden disk. The fifteenth-century artist Masaccio, in his Brancacci Chapel frescoes in Florence, broke the mold by putting halos in perspective so that they worked within the overall composition of the painting.

Early Madonnas

Botticelli's earliest works in Florence showed how much he had absorbed from Lippi. Several Madonnas (depictions of the Virgin Mary) offer proof of this link between the two painters. The coloring and positioning of Mary and assorted angels and saints echo the work of Lippi, in particular his *Madonna and Child with Two Angels* (see page 9). Botticelli also used Lippi's technique of contrasting light fabrics such as Mary's transparent veil with darker-colored fabrics such as the Virgin's dress. But even in these paintings, Botticelli is beginning to develop his own style, preferring cleaner, slender lines.

Andrea del Verrocchio

The workshop, or bottega, of Andrea del Verrocchio (1435–88) was the training ground for some of Italy's greatest artists, notably Leonardo da Vinci (1452–1519) and Domenico Ghirlandaio (1449–94). Botticelli went there when he returned to Florence in 1467. Art historians cannot agree on the exact role Botticelli played in this workshop, either continuing his apprenticeship or contributing as an artist in his own right. It does seem clear, however, that he played a part in some of the collaborative works produced by this prolific workshop. It is likely that Botticelli and Leonardo each painted an angel on the famous *Baptism of Christ* (see page 24).

▶ *Verrocchio's drawing,* Head of an Angel *(c. 1470). Verrocchio trained as a goldsmith, found fame as a sculptor and painter, and is remembered as one of the most important teachers of the Renaissance.*

Antonio del Pollaiuolo

Antonio del Pollaiuolo (c. 1433–98), like Verrocchio, had experience as a goldsmith, sculptor, and painter and was an important master. With his younger brother Piero (1443–96), he produced a range of works in gold, sculpture, and other decorative works. Some historians speculate that Botticelli might have worked at their workshop briefly. Pollaiuolo's own works reflect a robust awareness of movement and perspective, and many have classical themes.

▶ Hercules and Antaeus *(c. 1475) is Antonio Pollaiuolo's sculpted replica of a large painting created for Lorenzo the Magnificent, which is now lost. Of the same composition, Pollaiuolo did a copy on a very small panel, now kept at the Uffizi, the most important art gallery in Florence.*

Lippi in Spoleto

Fra Filippo Lippi's work in Spoleto was to prove his greatest and final commission. He was contracted to paint a series of frescoes in the spacious apse of the Cathedral of Santa Maria. He expanded, and in some cases replaced, works dating back to the cathedral's rebuilding in the thirteenth century. Lippi devoted himself to this series of scenes from the life of Mary, much to the pleasure of his patrons, the cathedral commissioners. The work, however, was incomplete when Lippi died unexpectedly in 1469.

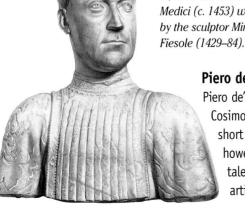

◀ *This bust of Piero de' Medici (c. 1453) was created by the sculptor Mino da Fiesole (1429–84).*

▶ *This detail from Lippi's Santa Maria frescoes in Spoleto shows Mary at the time of the Annunciation.*

Piero de' Medici

Piero de' Medici (1416–69) succeeded his father, Cosimo (1389–1464), but his rule was cut short by ill health. By the time of his death, however, it seems that he had recognized the talent of Botticelli and was probably the artist's first Medici patron.

Going It Alone

1469 After the death of Piero de' Medici, his son, Lorenzo (the Magnificent) becomes ruler of Florence.

1470 Commissioned by the Sei della Mercanzia, Botticelli completes the allegorical painting *Fortitude*.

Verrocchio, with the help of his assistants (Leonardo da Vinci and possibly Botticelli), paints the *Baptism of Christ*.

1472 Botticelli registers in the guild list of the Compagnia degli Artisti di San Luca (Artists' Guild of Saint Luke).

1477–80 The Sistine Chapel is built in the Vatican.

In 1470, Botticelli set up his own workshop in his father's house in Florence. One of the first major commissions — to paint the virtue of Fortitude for the Merchants' Guild — might have owed something to the support of his former neighbors, the influential Vespucci family. In 1472, Botticelli registered in the guild list of the Compagnia degli Artisti di San Luca. In a neat reversal of family roles, Fra Filippo's son, Filippino Lippi, appears in the same list as Botticelli's apprentice.

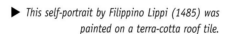

▶ *This self-portrait by Filippino Lippi (1485) was painted on a terra-cotta roof tile.*

Filippino

Fra Filippo Lippi was a worldly man who scandalized Florence with his love affair with the nun Lucrezia Buti. The two were released from their vows after Lucrezia gave birth to their son Filippino (1457–1504). When Filippo died in 1469, Filippino was put in the care of Fra Diamante (1430–98), Filippo's assistant, who completed the Spoleto frescoes. Upon returning to Florence, Filippino studied under Botticelli and went on to make his own name as an inventive and successful painter.

The Judith Panels

In about 1470, Botticelli painted two small panels with scenes from the tale of Judith. This Old Testament heroine was a favorite subject for Florentine artists, who saw her as a symbol of female strength. Judith had slain Holofernes, the Assyrian king's commander in chief, and returned his severed head to the Hebrews. This act of selfless courage appealed to Florentines, who saw their republic as being similarly threatened by hostile neighbors. The size of the panels — about 1 foot (31 cm) high — suggests that they were meant to be carried in special cases rather than hung.

◀ *In* The Return of Judith *(c. 1470), the heroine's maid, Abra, carries Holofernes' head while Judith holds an olive branch that symbolizes the peace she has won for her people.*

▶ *A relief sculpture on the bell tower of Florence Cathedral depicts the virtue of Justice.*

Virtues and Vices

European painting since the Middle Ages was steeped in a tradition of portraying human qualities in symbolic terms. Painters and sculptors used images of the human form — almost always female — to personify these attributes. The human qualities most commonly portrayed were known collectively as Virtues and Vices. Paintings, busts, and architectural motifs depicted virtues such as Faith, Hope, and Charity as well as Prudence, Justice, Fortitude, and Temperance. Renaissance artists continued the tradition but found themselves less constrained by the Church, so they felt able to feature pagan classical imagery in their symbolism.

The Merchant's Guild

Fortitude and the other six virtues were intended as backrests for chairs in the Sei della Mercanzia courtroom. There they would serve as incentive and warning for both the judges and the judged. Botticelli probably competed with other artists for the commission.

Botticelli's *Fortitude*

Botticelli's first datable painting was *Fortitude*, commissioned by the Sei della Mercanzia, a tribunal of Medici-influenced judges who dealt with merchants' disputes. *Fortitude* was to be one of a series representing the theological and cardinal virtues. Piero del Pollaiuolo had been commissioned to paint all seven but had failed to complete the project in time. Possibly supported by Botticelli's neighbor, the influential Giorgio Antonio Vespucci, the relatively unknown artist was contracted to complete two.

▼ *Piero del Pollaiuolo's* Temperance *(1469–70) portrays a woman mixing wine with water.*

▶ *Botticelli's* Fortitude *(1470) was a triumph of his maturing style.*

1472 Botticelli's brother Antonio also enrolls in the Artists' Guild of Saint Luke.

c. 1473 Botticelli receives the commission to paint *Saint Sebastian*.

1474 Botticelli's *Saint Sebastian* is completed and hung in the church of Santa Maria Maggiore.

A Style Matures

Botticelli's painting *Fortitude* put the artist in the forefront of the burgeoning Florentine artistic world. Established in the public eye as well as among his peers (thanks to his membership in the Artists' Guild of Saint Luke), he could be assured of new commissions. In 1473, Botticelli received just such a commission. He was contracted to paint *Saint Sebastian* in the central nave of the Church of Santa Maria Maggiore.

Saint Luke

The evangelist Saint Luke has long been associated with medicine and was described by Saint Paul as the "beloved physician." Renaissance artists also portrayed him as an artist, based on legends that he had painted various icons of the Virgin Mary.

▲ *A detail of* Saint Luke Drawing the Virgin and Child *(1435) by the Flemish artist Rogier van der Weyden (1399–1464).*

◄ *Botticelli's* Saint Sebastian *(1473). This work was designed to decorate a church column, so the panel on which it was painted has a long, narrow shape.*

Saint Sebastian

Legend had it that the Roman Emperor Diocletian ordered archers to fire arrows at Saint Sebastian because of his Christian beliefs. Sebastian survived this gruesome test and throughout the Middle Ages became a favorite artistic subject. Over time, his ordeal became linked with the figurative arrows of the plague, with which God tested Man. Fifteenth-century Florence suffered from occasional epidemics of plague, and many paintings and shrines invoked Saint Sebastian's help.

The Plague in the Renaissance

Medicine was a poorly developed science in Medieval and Renaissance Florence. Most people associated serious epidemics of the plague and other diseases with some sort of punishment from God. By this reasoning, people believed that physical cures had to be part of a religious purging of communal sin. Confraternities — lay brotherhoods linked by a religious purpose — devoted themselves to the care of the sick, tending sufferers and ensuring that the dead had a Christian burial.

◄ *This detail of a fifteenth-century painting by an anonymous artist shows confraternity members carrying a sick man to a hospital.*

A Puzzling Portrait

By the early 1470s, Botticelli was establishing himself as a portrait painter. His subjects were members of the leading families of Florence. One of Botticelli's finest — and most puzzling — works is the *Portrait of a Young Man With a Medal*. Some critics believe the man to be a loyal Medici follower or a family relative. Other theories suggest that the sitter may a goldsmith showing off his creation — possibly Botticelli's brother, Antonio.

▶ Portrait of a Young Man With a Medal *(c. 1474). The subject is almost as mysterious as Leonardo's* Mona Lisa *(completed c. 1515).*

▲ *A vase from the collection of Lorenzo the Magnificent, who was a noted patron and collector.*

▶ *Commemorative medal (1480) by Niccolò Francesco di Spinelli showing the profile of Lorenzo the Magnificent.*

Renaissance Medals

Few other areas of artistic achievement link the Renaissance with the classical world as much as medal production. The Romans had commemorated their heroes and statesmen with coins featuring their likenesses. Seeing themselves as natural successors to the Romans, the rulers of Florence and other Italian city-states commissioned artists to create similar medals. Leading families, such as the Medici in Florence, had coins struck to honor themselves and to commemorate great military victories and other events. Some artists, notably Antonio Pisano (Il Pisanello, 1395–1455) of Verona, achieved fame largely through the medals they created.

Growing Fame

Botticelli's fame spread beyond his native Florence. In 1474, he was asked to do a sample fresco, *The Assumption of the Virgin,* for the Cathedral in Pisa. For some reason, this work did not lead to further commissions. Botticelli returned to Florence with the work unfinished and a renewed determination to succeed on home ground. His reputation and his links with the Medici family led the social climber Guasparre del Lama to commission *Adoration of the Magi,* featuring depictions of the Medici (and of Botticelli himself).

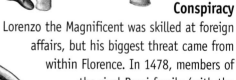

▼ *A detail from Gozzoli's* Adoration of the Magi *(c. 1460) featuring Medici portraits.*

Medici Pageantry

Fifteenth-century Florence cherished its republican tradition, but its leading family and de facto rulers, the Medici, lived and behaved like royalty. They commissioned works of art to reflect this elevated status. In 1459, Piero de' Medici chose Benozzo Gozzoli (1420–97) to paint a continuous fresco around the chapel in the Palazzo Medici. The theme — the Adoration of the Magi — reflected the Medici habit of staging processions in costume on the feast of the Epiphany.

▼ *A detail of* Portrait of Giuliano de' Medici *(c. 1478), painted near the time Giuliano was assassinated.*

Giuliano de' Medici

By the mid-1470s, Botticelli was one of the most widely regarded — and most influentially placed — artists in Florence. This position reflected his position as a favorite of the ruling Medici family. Giuliano (1453–78), the younger brother of the ruling Lorenzo, particularly favored Botticelli, commissioning portraits and in 1475 appearing at a civic tournament with a standard painted by Botticelli.

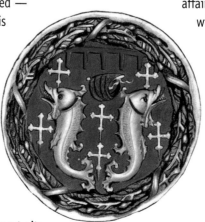

▲ *Coat of arms of the Pazzi family, rivals of the Medici for control of Florence.*

The Pazzi Conspiracy

Lorenzo the Magnificent was skilled at foreign affairs, but his biggest threat came from within Florence. In 1478, members of the rival Pazzi family (with the support of Pope Sixtus IV) attacked the Medici at Easter Mass in the Cathedral of Florence. Giuliano was killed, but the wounded Lorenzo survived to take revenge on the Pazzi and their followers.

▶ *A medal commemorating the Pazzi Conspiracy, featuring the image of Giuliano de' Medici.*

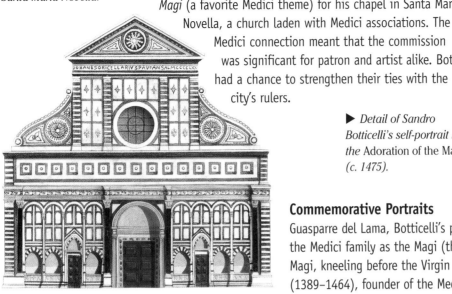

▼ *In 1470, Leon Battista Alberti completed the upper facade of the church of Santa Maria Novella.*

An Important Commission

In 1474, the rich and socially ambitious merchant Guasparre del Lama contracted Botticelli to paint the *Adoration of the Magi* (a favorite Medici theme) for his chapel in Santa Maria Novella, a church laden with Medici associations. The Medici connection meant that the commission was significant for patron and artist alike. Both had a chance to strengthen their ties with the city's rulers.

▶ *Detail of Sandro Botticelli's self-portrait in the* Adoration of the Magi *(c. 1475).*

Commemorative Portraits

Guasparre del Lama, Botticelli's patron, had the artist paint portraits of the Medici family as the Magi (the Three Wise Men). The eldest of the Magi, kneeling before the Virgin and the Christ Child, is Cosimo the Elder (1389–1464), founder of the Medici dynasty. Two figures look out at the observer from the right of the painting. The white-haired man in the blue robe is del Lama. To the far right is Botticelli himself.

▼ *The Adoration of the Magi (c. 1475), originally a chapel altarpiece in the church of Santa Maria Novella.*

The Wider Community

1480 Botticelli's tax declaration lists five assistants in his workshop.

Saint Augustine completed as a companion piece to Ghirlandaio's *Saint Jerome in his Study* at the church of Ognissanti.

1481 Botticelli completes an *Annunciation* for the hospital of San Martino della Scala, where victims of the plague are treated. It was commissioned in gratitude to Our Lady for delivering Florence from the plague that had swept through the city in 1478.

▼ *Pietà (c. 1480), a fresco by Domenico Ghirlandaio (1449–94) in the church of Ognissanti with portraits of members of the Vespucci family.*

Botticelli's relationship with the Medici family boosted his reputation within Florence. He now had works on display in two of the city's key buildings — the Merchants' Guild and the church of Santa Maria Novella. In 1480, the Vespucci family commissioned him to paint an allegorical Saint Augustine in another important building, the church of Ognissanti. The result was a triumph of devotional painting.

▼ *A portrait of Amerigo Vespucci at the Palazzo Farnese, Caprarola, showing the Florentine mariner examining the navigational maps that made him famous.*

Amerigo Vespucci

Amerigo Vespucci (1454–1512) was sent to Spain by Medici employers around the time of Christopher Columbus's first famous voyage. As navigator on Spanish and Portuguese voyages from 1497 to 1504, Vespucci discovered the Amazon, Orinoco, and Plate rivers. Moreover, he was the first European to describe these lands as new and not part of Asia. In 1507, the German scholar Martin Waldseemüller produced a world map describing these lands as "America" (from "Amerigo") for the first time.

The Vespuccis

Botticelli's wealthy neighbors, the Vespucci family, had risen to their powerful social position in the early 1400s. Shrewd business sense (they were wine merchants and later silk manufacturers) and loyalty to the Medici family combined to help the Vespuccis gain wealth and social standing. From 1434, members of the Vespucci family held high office in the Florentine republic.

Saving Frescoes

▲ *Botticelli's* Annunciation *(1481). Parts of the fresco are missing.*

Frescoes are created by painting directly on freshly laid plaster. Atmospheric conditions (mainly excessive humidity) or simply a weakening wall can endanger a fresco. Botticelli's *Saint Augustine* was removed from its original site in the church of Ognissanti in the 1500s when the wall was razed. Then, as now, restorers used techniques called *strappo* and *stacco*. Both methods use strong glue, which dries on the outer (colored) layer. The fresco is then pulled carefully off the original wall, treated to remove excess plaster, and then remounted. Some frescoes, like Botticelli's 1481 *Annunciation*, were moved from their original location and are now housed in museums.

▲ *Ghirlandaio's* Saint Jerome in his Study *(1480), the companion piece to Botticelli's* Saint Augustine.

Saint Augustine

The Vespuccis were instrumental in arranging Botticelli's commission for *Saint Augustine*. Appearing opposite — and identical in size to — Ghirlandaio's *Saint Jerome in his Study*, the painting shows Augustine at the moment of his vision of Jerome. Augustine was about to write to Jerome when the latter appeared to him, telling him of the impossibility of describing bliss. In fact, the vision came at the moment of Jerome's death, just before sunset. A prototype clock behind Augustine's head records the time of the vision.

▼ *"Where is Brother Marino" detail from* Saint Augustine. *Botticelli poked gentle fun at the monks of Ognissanti by inserting a snatch of their conversation in the page of Augustine's open book.*

Domenico Ghirlandaio

The church of Ognissanti already had a number of works by Domenico Ghirlandaio, notably the *Pietà* (opposite) and the *Madonna of Mercy*. In 1480, however, Ghirlandaio found himself working alongside Botticelli as the pair of artists created the frescoes of *Saint Jerome in his Study* and *Saint Augustine*. The frescoes were conceived of, and executed as, companion pieces and were originally placed on either side of the entrance to the monks' choir.

▼ *Saint Augustine (1480) by Botticelli. The artist captured Augustine's wonder as he was greeted by Jerome in a vision.*

▲ *Detail of* Saint Jerome in his Study *showing fifteenth-century writing tools on the desk.*

The Papal Request

1471–84 During the reign of Pope Sixtus IV, old buildings are razed and medieval streets are widened in Rome while ancient monuments are pillaged for building materials.

1481–2 With other leading artists, Botticelli is commissioned to paint in the new Sistine Chapel. In Rome, Botticelli becomes familiar with recently recovered classical statues.

1482 Botticelli's father dies in Florence.

In 1481, Pope Sixtus IV acknowledged Botticelli's reputation by summoning him to Rome to decorate the walls of the newly built Sistine Chapel. This great honor was shared by the artists Luca Signorelli, Cosimo Rosselli, Perugino, and Domenico Ghirlandaio. Botticelli's genius shines through his frescoes, despite their episodic nature. The Pope signaled his pleasure by paying Botticelli more than the other artists.

▶ *A portrait of Sixtus IV from the walls of the Sistine Chapel. Of the twenty-three remaining portraits that line the walls of the chapel, only seven have been attributed to Botticelli.*

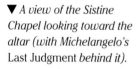
▶ *The coat of arms of the Della Rovere family.*

A Chapel for the Pope

Francesco Della Rovere (1414–84), a Franciscan, was elected pope in 1471, taking the name Sixtus IV. Although Sixtus was nominally subject to a vow of poverty, his thirteen-year papacy was noted for its violence, intrigue, and lavish spending. Sixtus IV elevated ill-suited relatives to the position of cardinal and supported the ill-fated Pazzi Conspiracy against the Medicis in 1478 (see page 16). His ambitious building plans aimed to raise Rome to the level of Florence, Venice, and other leading art centers. Chief among these plans was the construction of a chapel where the Church's most sacred rituals would take place and popes would be elected. Pope Sixtus IV summoned many of Italy's greatest artists to decorate the Sistine Chapel, which took its name from the Pope himself.

▼ *A view of the Sistine Chapel looking toward the altar (with Michelangelo's* Last Judgment *behind it).*

Other Artists at Work

Sixtus IV lavished Vatican funds to attract artists to his Sistine Chapel project. Luca Signorelli (c. 1445–1523), Cosimo Rosselli (1439–1507), Perugino (c. 1445–1523), and Domenico Ghirlandaio joined Botticelli in painting biblical scenes on the chapel walls. Undoubtedly the most famous work in the Sistine Chapel was later executed by Michelangelo (1475–1564), who was commissioned initially by Julius II (1443–1513), nephew of Sixtus IV, to paint the ceiling in 1508. From 1534 to 1541, Michelangelo painted the *Last Judgment* on the altar wall. Both projects involved painting over some of the work done in Botticelli's time.

▶ *Botticelli's* The Punishment of Korah, Dathan, and Abiram *(1481–2) shows Moses (center, with arm upstretched) punishing his rivals.*

▲ *Detail of a landscape showing Roman monuments from a fresco by Andrea Mantegna (1431–1506) from the Camera degli Sposi in Mantua.*

The City of Rome

Rome had been a source of inspiration for Renaissance artists eager to rediscover the past. The city itself, however, was hardly more than the sum of its ruins, with disorderly medieval buildings mingling with crumbling palaces and temples. It could hardly be compared with Florence and other thriving artistic centers in Italy in the fifteenth century. Within decades, however, a renewed papacy and a burgeoning merchant class had begun to transform Rome. Great artists were called to create new works rather than copy ancient ruins.

Botticelli in the Sistine Chapel

The Sistine artists were commissioned to paint a series of frescoes with scenes from the Old Testament and New Testament. Incidents from the life of Moses (seen as an Old Testament precursor of Jesus) shared space with events from Christ's life. Botticelli received a greater fee than the other artists. Besides the *The Punishment of Korah, Dathan, and Abiram,* Botticelli painted two other scenes: *Jewish Sacrifice* and the *Temptation of Christ.* The latter is a pictorial account of Christ's three main temptations by Satan.

▶ *The Arch of Constantine, typical of the monumental ruins that attracted Renaissance artists to Rome.*

Botticelli and Dante

Botticelli's connections with the Medici family led to a project that occupied the artist on and off for two decades. Upon Botticelli's return from Rome, Lorenzo di Pierfrancesco de' Medici (1463–1503), the cousin of Lorenzo the Magnificent, commissioned the artist to illustrate Dante's *The Divine Comedy*. Botticelli was entranced by the poet's account of a journey through Hell, Purgatory, and Paradise.

The Divine Comedy in the Renaissance

The epic poem *The Divine Comedy*, completed in 1321 by Dante Alighieri (1265–1321), tells how the Latin poet Virgil (70 B.C.–19 B.C.) guides Dante through Hell and Purgatory. Virgil, a pagan, cannot lead Dante into Paradise, but the task is undertaken by Beatrice, a woman Dante had loved as an adolescent. Written in vernacular Italian rather than Latin, it was hailed as a milestone. In 1481, the Florentine humanist Cristoforo Landino (1424–92) undertook to print and commission illustrations for the epic poem, which is made up of one hundred cantos, or sections.

▲ *An illustration of part II of Canto XV of Dante's Purgatorio, the second part of* The Divine Comedy, *by an anonymous fifteenth-century Lombard artist.*

▼ Dante and His Poem *(1465), by Domenico di Michelino (1417–91), probably inspired some of Botticelli's illustrations for* The Divine Comedy.

▲ Inferno XVIII, *now in the Berlin State Museums, shows how Botticelli imagined Virgil and Dante in Hell watching souls being tortured by devils.*

Botticelli's Drawings

Botticelli was commissioned to provide manuscript illustrations for each of the one hundred cantos of *The Divine Comedy*. He also provided designs for nineteen copper engravings for the first nineteen cantos. He probably did the engraving designs first because the drawings show how some of the ideas developed visually. Working with a lead stylus on large sheets of parchment, Botticelli completed the illustrations in ink. For some reason, the manuscript illustrations were left incomplete. By the seventeenth century, the collection had been split up. Some ninety-two survive in two collections, one in Berlin and one in the Vatican.

Dante, Beloved Florentine

Dante Alighieri had been inspired to write *The Divine Comedy* because of the infighting that convulsed his native Florence (and much of Italy) in the Middle Ages. His tale was one of exile and a hope for return. Dante himself died in exile in Ravenna, but his memory is still held sacred by the people of Florence.

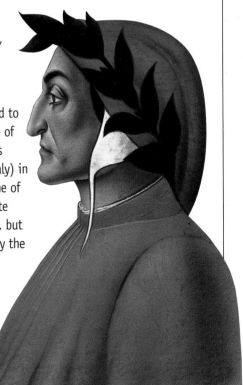

▶ *Botticelli's famous* Portrait of Dante *(c. 1490–5). The laurels on Dante's head are an echo of Domenico di Michelino's similar treatment (opposite).*

▲ *A detail from one of Botticelli's illustrations, now in the Vatican, shows a clearer view of the two poets, Virgil and Dante.*

Botticelli's Mythologies

c. 1478–82 Botticelli works on his masterpiece *Primavera*, although no one can now be sure exactly where, when, and for whom he completed the work.

1482 Lorenzo di Pierfrancesco de' Medici commissions Botticelli to paint *Pallas and the Centaur*. Marsilio Ficino writes *Platonic Theology*, a philosophical study of the soul. Leonardo da Vinci goes to Milan.

Botticelli's stay in Rome had confirmed his position as one of Italy's leading religious painters, but the trip had some additional benefits. Living and working among the classical Roman ruins, Botticelli had enhanced his own appreciation of the pagan stories and images. These underpinned the mythology that Renaissance humanists were happy to use (alongside more traditional Christian themes) to champion the cause of Neoplatonism. Botticelli found a new freedom to include a wider range of symbols in his visual imagery. This freedom in turn led to some of the most cherished paintings of the Renaissance.

▶ *The pose of Botticelli's Pallas was similar to that of Verrocchio's John the Baptist in the* Baptism of Christ *(1475–8).*

▶ Pallas and the Centaur *(c. 1482). Botticelli used classical themes and imagery to depict the triumph of virtue over sensuality.*

Pallas and the Centaur

Lorenzo di Pierfrancesco de' Medici had become an ardent patron of Botticelli by the early 1480s. In 1482, he commissioned Botticelli to paint a representation of Pallas Athena (goddess of wisdom, virtue, and beauty) restraining the centaur, who symbolizes all that is worldly and base in human nature. Botticelli, with his newfound interest in classical mythology, used pagan figures to represent a theme that could equally have been expressed in Christian terms. Giorgio Vasari (1511–74) reported that the painting resembled the now-lost standard that Botticelli had painted for Giuliano de' Medici in 1475 (see page 16). Botticelli wove diamond rings (Medici emblems) into the fabric of Pallas's garments.

The *Primavera* and Neoplatonism

Botticelli's patrons were strongly inspired by Neoplatonism. This humanist school of thought prized the passage from carnal love to a higher plane of reason and contemplation. Botticelli's great *Primavera* (Spring) is a prime example of the depiction of this theme. Laced with classical symbolism, the painting explores the spiritual and sensual as if in a graceful dance. But critics have struggled for centuries to unravel its exact meaning. Even its origin — long thought to have been commissioned by Lorenzo the Magnificent — has been thrown into doubt.

◀ *Detail from* Primavera *(c. 1478–82) showing the classical figures Zephyr and Chloris, inspired by Venus and Cupid to give birth to Flora.*

▼ *Detail of a Ghirlandaio fresco from Santa Maria Novella showing Marsilio Ficino (far left), Angelo Poliziano (second from right), and other leading scholars.*

Classical Sources

The Neoplatonist poet Angelo Poliziano is believed to have inspired much of the imagery in Botticelli's *Primavera*. But Poliziano in turn had looked further back to the classical period — to the hymns of Homer (ninth or eighth century B.C.), the odes of Horace (65–27 B.C.), and the work of Ovid (43 B.C.–A.D. 17) — for the first works praising the victory of intellect over instinct. Botticelli peoples the picture with familiar classical characters such as Venus, Mercury, and the Three Graces to strengthen this connection with the ancient world.

◀ *A Roman copy of a Greek depiction of the Three Graces (Aglaia, Euphrosyne, and Thalia), the smiling retinue of Venus.*

Springtime in Bloom

Botticelli's *Primavera* was not merely symbolic of spring and rebirth. Its imagery bursts with freshness and new growth, suggesting an idealized spring. But Flora's birth is accompanied by real flora. Art scholars have identified almost 500 species of plant, 190 of them flowers, at the feet of the characters depicted.

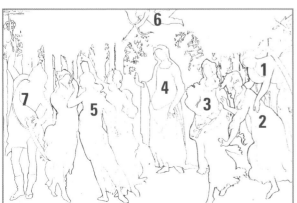

▶ *Detail of the flowers depicted at the feet of Flora and Venus in Botticelli's* Primavera.

◀ *The main figures in* Primavera *(see pages 26–27) are believed to be (1) Zephyr, (2) Chloris, (3) Flora, (4) Venus, (5) The Three Graces, (6) Cupid, and (7) Mercury.*

Botticelli's Mythologies

▶ Primavera *(c. 1478–82).*
Although mystery
surrounds this painting, it
is one of Botticelli's most
famous works. To this
day, it attracts millions of
visitors to the Uffizi
Gallery in Florence, where
it has hung since 1919.

1482 The Dominican friar Girolamo Savonarola arrives in Florence from Ferrara but does not become a major force for several years.

c. 1482 Filippino Lippi, by this time working independently, completes the fresco cycle depicting the story of the life of St. Peter in the Brancacci chapel in the church of Santa Maria del Carmine left unfinished in the 1420s by Masaccio (1401–28) and Masolino da Panicale (1383–1440). One of the figures in the scene of the Crucifixion of Peter is thought by some to be a portrait of Botticelli.

1482–5 Ghirlandaio paints in the Sassetti chapel in the church of Santa Trinità.

A Classical Masterpiece

Today, Botticelli's *Primavera* hangs in Florence's Uffizi Gallery with another of the artist's renowned classical masterpieces, *The Birth of Venus*. It seems obvious, in stylistic terms, that the two paintings were completed at about the same time. *The Birth of Venus* yields its symbolic secrets more readily, but this great work still has its mysteries. The title (dating from the nineteenth century) is misleading because we see not Venus's birth but her arrival on dry land on the island of Kythera (Cyprus).

Modest Venus

Botticelli was acknowledging the classical artistic tradition in the pose he chose for Venus (the Roman name for the Greek Aphrodite). Greek and Roman sculptors had celebrated Venus's chastity and purity by emphasizing her modesty. In a classical style of sculpture known as the Venus *pudica* (Modest Venus), she was shown covering her nakedness. One hand stretched across her naked breasts, while the other (helped in the case of Botticelli's painting by luxurious tresses) covered her pubic area.

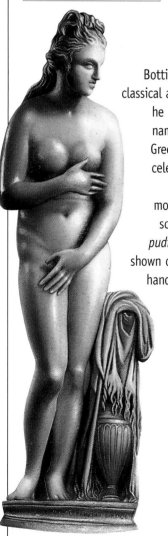

◀ The Capitoline Venus *(a Roman copy of a classical Greek work) is an example of the Venus pudica. Botticelli would have seen similar sculptures during his time in Rome and in the art collections in Florence.*

▲ Villa di Castello *(1599–1602) by the sixteenth-century artist Justus van Utens. By the early fifteenth century,* The Birth of Venus *formed part of the furnishings of this Medici villa.*

The Myth of Hesiod

The great Greek poet Homer (ninth or eighth century B.C.) described Aphrodite as the daughter of Zeus and Dione, but few legends grew from this story. It seems likely that Botticelli and contemporary Renaissance scholars preferred the account given by Hesiod (eighth century B.C.). In his version, Cronus castrated his father Uranus and cast his genitals into the sea. They floated and produced a foam (*aphros* in Greek), from which Aphrodite arose. Zephyr, the West Wind, blew her gently to the shores of Kythera (Cyprus). There she was greeted by the Three Graces, who clothed her, gave her jewels, and escorted her to the assembly of the immortals. Botticelli captured Venus (Aphrodite) just as she reached dry land.

▶ *An ancient Greek hydria (urn) decorated with images of the birth of Aphrodite.*

◀ The Birth of Venus *(c. 1485). Botticelli based Venus's pose on classical sculptures of Aphrodite.*

The Birth of Venus

In strictly mythological terms, Botticelli depicted Venus's arrival, not her birth. But his composition, with its biblical echoes, suggests Christian Baptism, or spiritual birth. Mingling pagan and Christian symbols would have appealed to Neoplatonists such as Lorenzo di Pierfrancesco de' Medici. The painting (along with *Primavera*) was listed in the inventory of the Villa di Castello (Lorenzo's residence) in 1558, but it does not appear in the inventory of 1499. Unlike *Primavera*, which was painted on a rich wood panel, *The Birth of Venus* was painted on canvas, which made it possible for its owner to take it with him on his travels or whenever he moved from his city residence to his villa in the country. Perhaps it was intended for someone's "home away from home," but it still is not certain whose.

Courtly Love and War

Venus and Mars

The story of Venus and Mars (originally named Aphrodite and Ares by the Greeks) was a popular — if lewd — theme for paintings celebrating weddings. Botticelli depicts the goddess of love lying with the sleeping god of war just before the pair is caught by Venus's jealous husband Hephaistos. War has been conquered by Love, and the playful satyrs toy with Mars's weapons. Botticelli includes a nest of wasps (*vespe* in Italian) by the head of Mars. This is probably a pun on the name of his likely patrons, the Vespucci family.

▶ Venus and Mars *(c. 1483). The amorous couple is lying in a grove of myrtles, trees that were always associated with Venus.*

By the early 1480s, Botticelli had developed a distinctive, successful style that was equally at home with portraiture, classical allusion, and devotional imagery. His work was suffused with the Neoplatonist spirit of the age so cherished by the Florentine leading families who were now his patrons. Botticelli's masterful *Venus and Mars* plays with themes he had developed in *Primavera* and *The Birth of Venus*, adding some contemporary fifteenth-century touches and even an allusion to his likely patron.

▼ Ariadne Sleeping *(ancient Greek). Botticelli is believed to have seen a similar sculpture while working in Rome, later modeling his figures after ancient works.*

Renaissance Games

The mischievous satyrs in Botticelli's *Venus and Mars* have taken hold of the helmet and lance of the god of war and turned them into playthings. The weapon and armor had no real equivalent in classical Greece or Rome: Botticelli is actually depicting the sort of weapon that fifteenth-century Italians would recognize from tournaments in the great squares of their cities. The tournaments comprised mainly jousting competitions between knights and soldiers of noble birth, carrying on a European tradition that dated back to the Middle Ages. The contests were popular spectator sports, and many participants decked themselves out in spectacular costumes. It was at one such tournament in 1475 that Giuliano de' Medici carried a standard painted by Botticelli. The popularity of tournaments died away during the fifteenth century as firearms replaced traditional chivalric weapons.

▼ Cleopatra *(c. 1480) by Piero di Cosimo (1462–1521). This work was once believed to be the portrait of Simonetta Vespucci.*

▲ Joust with Horses in Piazza Santa Croce *(school of Vasari, sixteenth century). This spacious square was a popular venue for Renaissance tournaments.*

Simonetta Vespucci

The beauty of Simonetta Vespucci (c. 1454–76), born Simonetta Cattaneo, captivated much of Florence during her short life. She married Marco Vespucci, a distant cousin of Amerigo, but the Medici menfolk also seemed to be smitten by her. Some say that Simonetta was the mistress of Giuliano, brother of Lorenzo the Magnificent. Her beauty is thought to have inspired Botticelli in his allegorical paintings (notably *The Birth of Venus*) and in the depictions of Mary in some religious works.

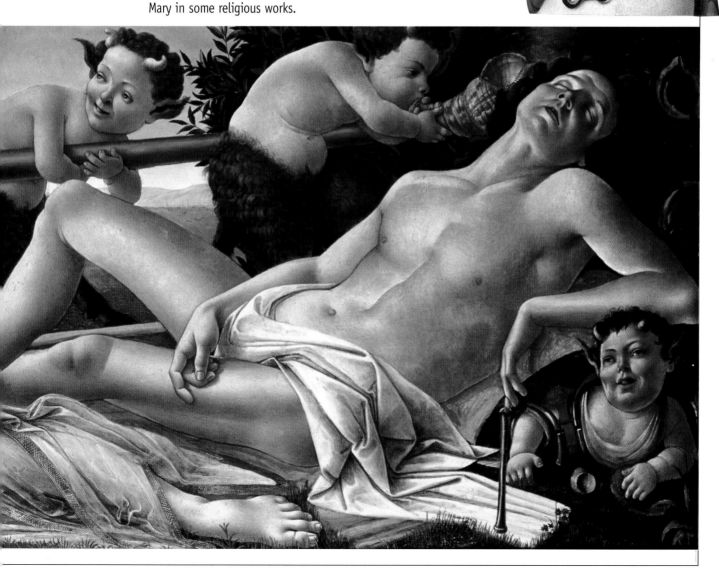

1483 Botticelli completes drawings and supervises his students in the completion of four panels celebrating the wedding of Giannozzo Pucci and Lucrezia Bini.

1484 Pope Innocent VIII succeeds Sixtus IV. Botticelli believes he is still owed money from the Sistine Chapel commission.

1485 Commissioned by Giovanni d'Agnolo de' Bardi, Botticelli completes an altarpiece in the church of Santo Spirito.

1486 Giovanni Tornabuoni commissions Botticelli to paint frescoes in a villa.

The Domestic Realm

▶ *A portrait of the scholarly Boccaccio by Andrea del Castagno (1423–57).*

Botticelli's rendering of love and tenderness made him an obvious choice of artist for wealthy patrons intent on decorating their homes with the latest — and most highly esteemed — works of art. Prosperous urban Italians of the fifteenth century lived in considerable comfort. Great homes and palaces no longer needed a defensive function, so the wealthy were free to decorate them as they pleased. Some of the most highly prized works of art were commissioned for bedrooms, the most private of all rooms.

Boccaccio

The poet Giovanni Boccaccio (1313–75) was born eight years before the death of Dante, and many Italians see him as a worthy successor to the author of *The Divine Comedy*. Along with fellow Florentine Petrarch (1304–74), Boccaccio used the vernacular Italian tongue to produce memorable poetry. His most famous work, *Decameron*, comprised one hundred comic and tragic tales written in pure and elegant Italian. Although completed in 1353, *Decameron* was not printed until 1470.

Nuptial Panels

About the time he completed *Venus and Mars*, Botticelli painted four panels depicting tales from Boccaccio's *Decameron*. They concern the story of Nastagio degli Onesti, a knight from Ravenna who loses, then regains, his beloved's heart. The wealthy merchant Antonio Pucci commissioned the panels to celebrate the wedding of his son Giannozzo to Lucrezia Bini. The wedding, said to have been negotiated by Lorenzo the Magnificent himself, was a social event of the highest order. Botticelli's panels were destined to be decorations in the couple's marriage chamber.

▼ *Botticelli's* The Banquet in the Pine Forest *(1482–3), the third episode from the tale of Nastagio degli Onesti.*

The Tornabuoni Family

The Tornabuoni family was one of the most influential in Florence. In 1486, Giovanni Tornabuoni (uncle of Lorenzo the Magnificent and head of the Rome branch of the Medici bank) is believed by some scholars to have commissioned Botticelli to paint a pair of frescoes. They were painted in Giovanni's country villa near Florence and are thought to commemorate the wedding of Giovanni's son Lorenzo to Giovanna Albizzi. The frescoes originally faced each other and depicted the bride and groom being welcomed into the realm of mythological and allegorical figures. Venus and the Three Graces receive Giovanna while Lorenzo is led into the circle of the Seven Liberal Arts.

▼ *Domenico Ghirlandaio's fresco portrait of Giovanni Tornabuoni by the main altar of Santa Maria Novella.*

Art in Florentine Homes

The Florentines devoted much of their energy to extolling the virtues of love and marriage. Botticelli's paintings of the 1480s, many commissioned by proud or ambitious fathers, often concerned such themes. Their romantic themes made them best suited for the most intimate parts of the house, the bedrooms and marriage chambers. But idealized views of women did not end at the marriage ceremony. A woman who had given birth was also the object of esteem, and the birth was as much of a triumph as the wedding itself. Special panels and decorative plates, commissioned by the mothers' male admirers (not always the husbands) honored these happy occasions.

▼ A Young Man being Introduced to the Seven Liberal Arts *(c. 1486). Some scholars think that this fresco by Botticelli, painted in the Tornabuoni country villa, depicts Lorenzo Tornabuoni.*

▲ *Nativity scene (c. 1450) from a* desco da parto *(commemorative birth plate) by an anonymous painter. It would have been used by a baby's mother as a table for food.*

Religious Themes

1487 Botticelli paints the *Madonna of the Pomegranate* (a tondo) to hang in the Palazzo Vecchio.

1488 Andrea del Verrocchio, Botticelli's second master, dies.

1489 The San Marco Coronation altarpiece is completed by Botticelli.

1489–90 Benedetto di Ser Giovanni Guardi commissions Botticelli to paint the Annunciation for the family chapel in the monastery church of Cestello (now Santa Maria Maddalena dei Pazzi) in Borgo Pinti, Florence.

1490 With Filippino Lippi, Perugino, and Domenico Ghirlandaio, Botticelli paints frescoes at the villa at Spedaletto for Lorenzo the Magnificent.

▶ *Detail of Botticelli's Sant'Ambrogio Altarpiece (c. 1467–70), showing St. Cosma, a Medici patron saint.*

For all his genius in depicting classical scenes with panache and mystery, Botticelli remained a devout Catholic who was inspired by his religious commissions. Yet another treatment of the Adoration of the Magi was completed while he was still in Rome in approximately 1481. It led to a series of other Madonnas and religious works later in the decade back in Florence.

Altarpieces for Florentine Churches

One of Botticelli's earliest altarpieces was commissioned in 1483 by Giovanni d'Agnolo de' Bardi for the chapel he had built in the church of Santo Spirito. Throughout the 1480s, Botticelli received more altarpiece commissions. The subject of such paintings — usually centering on the Virgin Mary — was strictly limited, but Botticelli was able to experiment with new techniques (adding extra gold for the San Marco Coronation commissioned for the Guild of Goldsmiths) or with mathematical designs (as in the geometric *Annunciation* of 1489–90).

Holy Conversation

Many Renaissance altarpieces featured a representation of saints known as the *sacra conversazione* ("holy conversation"). Saints were venerated partly because of their exemplary lives but also because worshipers believed that saints could intercede on their behalf. In such a "holy conversation" setting, the saints would appear standing (or more commonly, kneeling) together with the Virgin Mary, either as the Madonna with Child or at her Assumption or Coronation. The choice of saints is often a clue to the origin of the painting. Artists would juggle historical periods to include the patron saint of a city or church — or perhaps the saint after whom the donor was named.

▼ *The Guild of Apothecaries and Doctors probably commissioned* The Virgin and Child with Four Angels and Six Saints *(c. 1487), Botticelli's altarpiece for the church of San Barnaba.*

The *Tondo*

The *tondo* (Italian for "circle") was a type of round painting that developed in Florence during the fifteenth century. *Tondi* (plural of *tondo*) had themes similar to the *deschi da parto* (see page 33) in wealthy households. The Virgin and Child and the Adoration of the Magi were especially popular. Some *tondi* (such as the famous works by Michelangelo) were carved from wood or marble.

▼ *Detail of the* Madonna and Child with Stories from the Life of Saint Anne *(c. 1453) by Fra Filippo Lippi.*

▲ *A sad and contemplative Virgin is the focus of* Madonna of the Pomegranate *(1487).*

Symbols

Botticelli, like other Renaissance artists, was familiar with a range of symbols associated with classical and Christian imagery. The pomegranate, for example, signified the resurrected Christ, adding a new dimension to a painting of the Virgin and Child. It in turn dated from pagan associations with regeneration each spring.

▶ The Annunciation *(1489–90), shown here in its original frame, was intended for the Guardi family chapel. It is now housed in the Uffizi Gallery in Florence.*

The Annunciation

Botticelli produced his remarkable *Annunciation* for the relatively humble (by the standards of the artist's usual patrons) Benedetto di Ser Giovanni Guardi. The viewer's gaze is drawn in geometrical fashion by the lines on the floor to the meeting of the angel Gabriel's hand with Mary's and then beyond to a landscape in the distance. Leonardo da Vinci, in his *Treatise On Painting*, seemed to single Botticelli's *Annunciation* out for its improbable positioning of its figures. Leonardo, whose own art reflected his scientific observation of life, believed the angel to be driving Mary from her room. Instead, Mary's position shows that she is somewhat frightened by the angel's apparition, in a typically human fashion.

1470s Botticelli's early portraits include *Portrait of a Lady* (Smeralda Bandini?) (c. 1470–75), *Portrait of a young Man with a Medal* (c. 1475), and *Portrait of Giuliano de' Medici* (c. 1478).

1480s–90s Famous portraits from Botticelli's mature period include *Young Woman in Mythological Guise* (c. 1485), *Portrait of a Young Man* (c. 1485), another *Portrait of a Young Man* (1489–90), *Portrait of Michele Marullo* (c. 1496–7), and *Portrait of Lorenzo de' Lorenzi* (c. 1498).

Portraiture

We have come to recognize a Botticelli in melancholic religious works or by the almost mystical portrayals of classical beauty. However, in his lifetime, Botticelli built a reputation as a skilled portrait artist. He depicted Giuliano de' Medici in the 1470s, and throughout his career, he completed portraits of notable — and sometimes less well-known — Florentines. These works also allowed an outlet for an artist who constantly sketched in his own time.

▶ *The Medici Nero's Seal medallion (first century B.C.) worn by the model in Botticelli's painting.*

The Italian Tradition

Renaissance Italians extolled the virtues of beauty and womanhood, but their portraits of women showed that there were other considerations at work. A beautiful woman was an asset to a family, easing the path to a successful marriage and increased prestige. As a result, many such portraits aimed to display a family's wealth or lineage. Women were depicted wearing clothing or jewels bearing the family's coat of arms. In the example to the right, the young woman wears a gem from the Medici collection.

▼ Portrait of a Young Woman *(c. 1435) by Rogier van der Weyden (1399–1464), an example of Flemish three-quarter portrait pose.*

Portraits in the North

Portraits in Italy followed the example of Renaissance medals (see page 15) by presenting their subjects in profile. These poses allowed the artist to fill the painting with symbols and details of wealth and social standing, but the subject's essential character was masked by the formal stance. From the 1470s, however, Italian artists began following the example of Jan van Eyck (c. 1390–1441), Hans Memling (c. 1435–1494), and other Flemish artists by portraying their sitters in three-quarter or full-face poses. Botticelli's *Portrait of a Young Man Holding a Medal* (see page 15) was an early example.

◀ Young Woman in Mythological Guise *(1485), believed to be modeled on Simonetta Vespucci.*

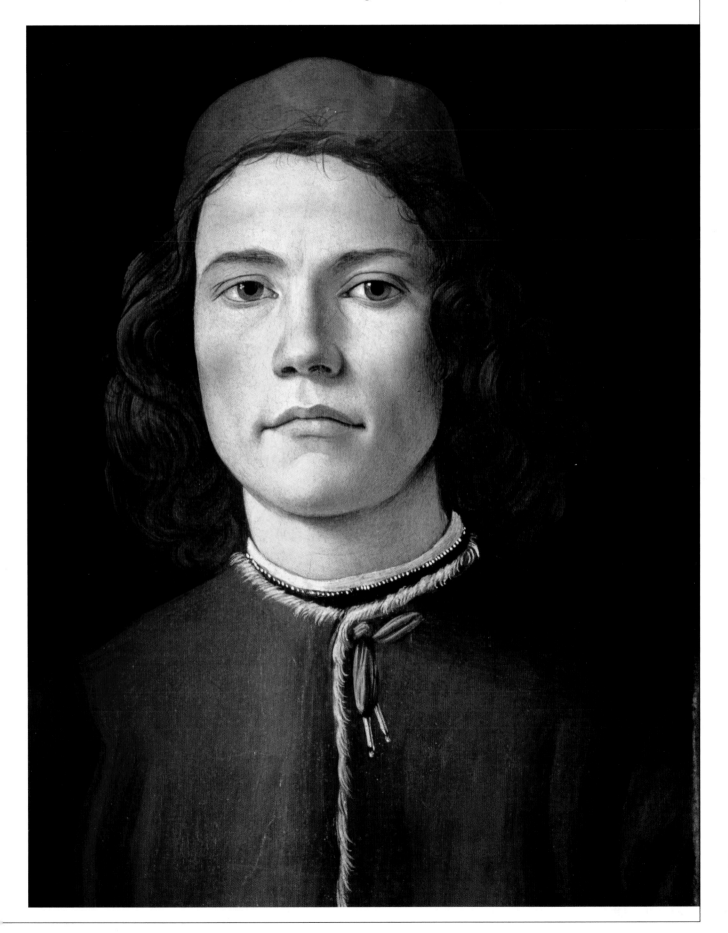

▼ *The subject of Botticelli's* Portrait of a Young Man *(1485) returns the gaze of the viewer directly because of the full-face pose. The man's simple clothing has led critics to believe he was one of the artist's assistants.*

An Austere Influence

Around the year 1494, a number of events strengthened the introspective melancholy that was always present in Botticelli's character. His works in the 1490s had begun to reflect an austere religious theme. These aspects of Botticelli's character developed further when the Medicis were expelled in 1494 and the fanatical monk Savonarola gained great power in Florence.

Botticelli and Apelles

Apelles (fourth century B.C.) was considered by his contemporaries to have been the greatest Greek painter in antiquity. Although written descriptions of his works fascinated Renaissance artists, none of his paintings survive. After Botticelli read the description of Apelles' painting *Calumny* in the writings of Lucian (c. 120–180) or in Leon Battista Alberti's *On Painting* (1436), he decided to recreate it. Botticelli's painting is a bitter reflection about unjust punishment caused by bad judgment, represented by King Midas flanked by Ignorance and Suspicion. The painting may refer to the violence and corruption in Florence's government at the time.

▼ The Calumny of Apelles *(c. 1495). An unjustly accused youth is being dragged to the king while Truth (far left) distances herself from the falsehoods.*

▲ *A relief depicting Apelles by Andrea Pisano (c. 1270–1348) once decorated the bell tower of Santa Maria del Fiore, the cathedral of Florence.*

▲ *Key to figures in* The Calumny of Apelles*: (1) King Midas, (2) Ignorance, (3) Suspicion, (4) Hatred, (5) Calumny, (6) Deceit, (7) Fraud, (8) the unjustly accused youth, (9) Remorse, and (10) Truth.*

Lamentation over the Dead Christ

Botticelli changed his style of painting dramatically in the 1490s, probably under the influence of Savonarola's message of austerity and piety. Gone were the graceful, flowing evocations of feminine beauty, complete with almost whimsical classical allusions. In their place came darker religious paintings that were suffused with sadness and suffering. *Lamentation over the Dead Christ* (c. 1495) was one of the first of these somber works.

Michelangelo

The great sculptor Michelangelo Buonarroti (1475–1564) was at the start of his illustrious career at the time when Savonarola's influence dominated Florence. Michelangelo would have been familiar with the works of Botticelli, and the reference to the older artist's style is evident in some of Michelangelo's work.

▶ *The elongated limbs and posture of Michelangelo's* Pietà *(1499) echo the composition of Botticelli's work.*

Fra Girolamo Savonarola in Florence

Fra Girolamo Savonarola (1452–98) was a reforming Dominican preacher whose message swept through Florence in the 1490s. Savonarola began as a lecturer in Florence in the early 1480s, but a Saul-like revelation in 1485 led him to travel around Tuscany, forcefully arguing that the corrupt Church needed reforming in order to be renewed. Savonarola targeted the pagan humanism of the day and also criticized the extravagant lives led by the Medicis and other leading families.

Botticelli, possibly through his brother Simone, seems to have followed the teachings of Savonarola. His paintings became darker and less concerned with feminine beauty.

◀ *Medal portrait of Savonarola, who became de facto ruler of Florence in 1494 when the Medicis were driven out by the French.*

▼ Lamentation over the Dead Christ *(c. 1495). Botticelli distorted the human shapes to add tension to the tragic scene.*

Mystical Repentance

Many of Botticelli's later religious works reflect the feelings of imminent destruction that so often swept through Europe at the ends of centuries. The end of the world and the Last Judgment seemed to be close at hand, prompting people into self-reproach. Botticelli's own character already had a deep vein of melancholy, and the spiritual turmoil of the Savonarola years resonated in his heart. His devotional paintings of this period reflect these concerns and seem far removed from the airy treatments he gave them in his earlier work. His art is no longer driven by gentle curves and light colors. Instead, a harsh angularity lies at the heart of the paintings. Sadness and repentance prevail in these later works.

Archaic Forms

In the later years of his career, Botticelli adopted a kind of archaic style, closer to that of painters of the early fifteenth century, as in his *Mystic Nativity*. Stylistically and thematically, the work echoes Fra Angelico's *Last Judgment*. Botticelli's intentions lie in the Greek inscription along the top (making it Botticelli's only signed work). He refers to Italy's recent time of troubles and cites St. John's *Revelation*. We can see Mary (the largest figure in the picture) as representing the Church. The embracing angels and humans hope and pray for the peace that will banish the devil (lower left) forever.

Savonarola's Preaching

Savonarola's preaching against tyranny and the wickedness of the ruling classes attracted a great deal of support, especially among the lower classes of Florentine society. They willingly participated in Savonarola's famous "bonfire of vanities" (destruction of unnecessary extravagances, including some works of art). Savonarola also bred enemies, notably King Charles VIII of France (1470–98) and Pope Alexander VI (1431–1503). In 1498, opponents of Savonarola stormed San Marco and captured him. After a brief trial, he was hanged and burned.

▼ *A 1495 woodcut of an impassioned Fra Girolamo Savonarola preaching in the Cathedral of Florence.*

▼ The Last Judgment *(c. 1432–5) by Fra Angelico. This panel was painted as a backrest of a priest's seat for the convent of Santa Maria degli Angeli in Florence.*

▼ Mystic Nativity *(c. 1501). Botticelli's abandonment of linear perspective in this work symbolized his view that the Renaissance had concentrated too much on science and not enough on piety.*

Last Years

Botticelli drew in on himself more as he became more concerned with spiritual matters. He withdrew from the forefront of the Florentine art world, which by now was championing new masters such as Michelangelo and Raphael. Largely ignored or forgotten in the new mood of naturalism, Botticelli worked less and less until his death.

▲ *A Florentine marriage chest from the 1470s. The chest is decorated with panels depicting familiar stories.*

Marriage Chests

Some of the finest Renaissance paintings decorated pieces of furniture in the homes of the wealthy. Such furniture also had a practical purpose (see *desco da parto*, page 33). *Cassoni* (marriage chests), containing cloth, clothing, and jewelry, were also decorated by the most established artists. Botticelli's *The Story of Lucretia* was one of a pair of panels most likely destined for such a marriage chest or for a headboard.

▼ The Story of Lucretia *(c. 1504). In the scene on the far left, Lucretia is threatened by Sextus. Lucius Junius Brutus finds her unconscious on the far right and calls on the army to take revenge after her suicide, center.*

The Story of Lucretia

The story of Lucretia concerns a young woman from ancient Rome who was raped by Sextus, the son of King Tarquin, and killed herself to save her family's honor. Lucius Junius Brutus then flamed a revolt against the king. Botticelli's depiction of the story alludes to contemporary events in Florence: the banishing of the Medicis and the restoration of the Florentine republic. He even included a representation of David, a symbol of republican Florence, standing on the column in the center of the scene.

▲ Four Scenes from the Early Life of Saint Zenobius *(c. 1500–5) shows (from left) Zenobius refusing to marry, his baptism, his mother's baptism, and his appointment as Bishop of Florence.*

▶ *A relief of Saint Zenobius (with Episcopal miter and crosier and showing Florence in the background) from the walls of Palazzo Vecchio.*

The Stories of Saint Zenobius

Zenobius (died c. 417) was the first bishop of Florence, where he became renowned for his preaching and austerity. A number of miracles were ascribed to Zenobius, leading to his canonization and to the continuing reverence in which he was held by the Florentines. A cult of Zenobius developed in the fifteenth century when his relics were returned to the main chapel in the Cathedral choir. In 1491, work began to decorate this choir, and Botticelli was one of the artists taking part. A description of Zenobius, published in 1487, was the probable source for the four panels Botticelli painted from about 1500 to 1505. The panels might well have decorated the walls of a religious confraternity in Florence.

Botticelli's Death

It is likely that the panels depicting scenes from the life of Saint Zenobius were the last works completed by Botticelli. By the start of the sixteenth century, he was nearing sixty, and he was becoming frail and crippled. He also played much less of a public role, although he did sit on the committee that decided where to place Michelangelo's heroic statue of *David* (1501–4). Botticelli died in May 1510 and was buried in the graveyard near the church of Ognissanti.

◀ *The Church of Ognissanti, Florence. Buildings now stand on the site of the nearby graveyard where Botticelli was buried.*

Botticelli's Renaissance

1512 Michelangelo completes the frescoes on the Sistine Chapel ceiling.

1848 A group of young English artists form the Pre-Raphaelite Brotherhood, adhering to a style of painting that owes a great deal to Botticelli.

1859 Sir Edward Coley Burne-Jones makes the first of four visits to Italy, where he admires the work of Botticelli and other Renaissance artists.

1873 The English art critic Walter Pater publishes *Studies in the History of the Renaissance*, which includes an important essay on the then-overlooked Botticelli.

c. 1895 The Art Nouveau art gallery opens in Paris, giving its name to an artistic style inspired by Botticelli.

1982 Botticelli's *Primavera* is restored.

▶ The Virgin and Child with Saint Anne *(c. 1510) by Leonardo da Vinci.*

▼ *An Art Nouveau theater poster for the actress Sarah Bernhardt (1897) by Alphonse Mucha (1860–1939).*

By the end of his life, Botticelli found that his style of painting — blending graceful wavy lines with new developments in perspective and composition — had fallen from favor. The Italian Renaissance was entering another phase, led by Leonardo, Michelangelo, and Raphael. Anatomy and a scientific approach to light and space were the order of the day, and Botticelli's work was considered archaic. His contributions to Western art were largely ignored for more than three centuries before being rediscovered dramatically. Botticelli's own "renaissance" saw his work inspiring new movements in European art.

Art Nouveau

The Art Nouveau movement, starting at the end of the nineteenth century and lasting to about 1910, was a reaction to the staid, historical art that had prevailed in previous decades. This "new art" (*art nouveau* in French) was originally decorative, but its sinuous lines (echoing some of Botticelli's *Primavera*-era paintings) found their way into architecture, furniture design, and even printing typefaces.

▶ *A portrait of John Ruskin by Sir John Everett Millais (1829—96).*

The High Renaissance Style

The High Renaissance style of the sixteenth century questioned some of the artistic and political "certainties" of the fifteenth century. Christianity was split by the Reformation, Rome was sacked in 1527, and the Florentine Republic fell in 1530. Artists struggled to deal with the turmoil around them. Botticelli's *Primavera* and *The Birth of Venus* seemed hopelessly out of date, but his last works, with their distorted and elongated shapes, actually prefigured some of the later developments often described as Mannerism.

John Ruskin

John Ruskin (1819–1900) was the most important British art critic of the nineteenth century. His devotion to the history of European art helped his generation rediscover and reassess many of the great Renaissance artists. Ruskin and his Swiss counterpart Jacob Burckhardt (1818–97) gave the term "Renaissance" its current meaning. Ruskin and the Pre-Raphaelites helped rescue Botticelli's reputation from obscurity.

▲ Lorenzo and Isabella *(1849) by Sir John Everett Millais. The subject and treatment echo the works of Botticelli.*

▶ The Garden of the Hesperides *(1870–3) by Sir Edward Coley Burne-Jones. The women's pose is a reference to the Three Graces in Botticelli's Primavera.*

The Pre-Raphaelites

The Pre-Raphaelite Brotherhood was a group of young British artists founded in 1848. The leading members were Sir John Everett Millais (1829–96), William Holman Hunt (1827–1910), and Dante Gabriel Rossetti (1828–82). Along with sympathetic critics such as John Ruskin, they reacted to what they saw as the stagnant state of art because of its slavish following of the academic tradition. They called for a simpler, more direct style of art that died away at about the time of Raphael (1483–1520). The Pre-Raphaelites painted works of uplifting or allegorical character inspired by close examination of the world around them.

Sir Edward Coley Burne-Jones

Sir Edward Coley Burne-Jones (1833–98) was a British painter, illustrator, and designer. Although not an original member of the Pre-Raphaelite Brotherhood, he was greatly inspired by Dante Gabriel Rossetti's work. Burne-Jones followed Rossetti's example of painting in the aesthetic ("art for art's sake") style, but he was particularly inspired by the works of Botticelli, whose elongated human forms inspired much of Burne-Jones's work. Burne-Jones quickly gained national and international fame when he began exhibiting his works in earnest in 1877.

Glossary

allegory A story or painting in which characters or figures represent good and bad qualities.

apprenticeship The hiring of a person under agreement to serve, for a specified period of time, a person skilled in a trade, for low wages. In the Renaissance, young boys seeking to become artists received their training by serving as apprentices in the workshops of established artists.

Art Nouveau An ornamental style of European and U.S. art that lasted from 1890 to 1910, characterized by the use of long, curving lines based on plant forms. This so-called "new" style (the word nouveau means "new" in French) was applied primarily to architecture, interior design, jewelry, glass design, and illustration.

attributed Credited an artist with the creation of a work of art.

calumny The act of falsely accusing someone, or an unjust statement made with the intention of destroying a person's reputation.

canto A main division of a long poem.

cassone An Italian word used to describe a wooden chest used to store a bride's dowry, such as household linens. *Cassoni* (plural of *cassone*) were often carved or decorated with paintings.

choir Part of the church building where the main altar is located. In the past, the choir was reserved for monks and priests.

classical Term used to describe works of art from ancient Greece or Rome or works that have the same characteristics as the works of ancient Greece or Rome.

commission The act of appointing someone to do a specified task, or the actual task or duty given to someone under an agreement, especially in terms of creating a work of art.

compagnia An Italian term used to describe an association, guild, or confraternity representing a certain trade.

composition The arrangement of the parts of something. The term is used to refer to the way in which objects are arranged, usually in a painting or sculpture.

confraternity A brotherhood or association of men united for some worthy purpose, usually a religious charity organization of lay members.

de facto Latin term meaning in fact but not necessarily according to law.

draftsman A person who is skilled in the art of drawing.

epic A long poem that celebrates the deeds of a heroic figure from history or tradition.

excommunication The act of punishing a member of the Catholic Church by forcing him or her out of active participation.

fresco painting A mural painting made by the application of color onto a wall when the top layer of plaster is still wet.

guild An association representing a trade or craft in medieval and Renaissance Europe.

humanism A cultural movement of the fifteenth century based on the study of classical texts, or a system of thought concerned with the needs of people rather than with those of religion.

joust A medieval sport that involved knights on horseback fighting with lances.

Mannerism An Italian art movement or style of the sixteenth century that broke away from the ideals of classical art with the distortion of forms and the use of bright colors.

Neoplatonism A school of ancient Greek philosophy (practiced in ancient times and later in the Renaissance) that revived the ideas of the philosopher Plato.

palazzo Italian word for building or palace.

patron A person who gives money to a person or group to perform a certain task or for some other worthy purpose. Patrons sometimes support artists and writers.

patron saint A holy man or woman who is believed to protect a particular group or community.

perspective The method of representing objects so as to make them appear three-dimensional. The illusion of depth and space or a view extending far into the distance.

Pietà Term used to refer to a work of art that depicts the Virgin Mary holding the dead body of Christ.

piety Deep respect and obedience to God or religion.

pigment Any substance, usually in the form of a fine powder, used as a coloring agent to make paint. A paint or dye.

Renaissance The cultural movement, originating in Italy during the fourteenth century and lasting until the seventeenth century, in which the art, literature, and ideas of ancient Greece were rediscovered and applied to the arts. The artistic style of this period.

restoration A process or act of bringing an object, work of art, or building back to its original state.

Ser An Italian title similar to "sir" in English.

standard A flag or banner carried at the top of a pole.

treatise A literary work, a book or article, in which an author expresses an opinion about a particular subject by examining its principles and treating them with a planned and organized discussion.

tyranny The use of cruel or unjust means by a ruler of a nation or group of people. An oppressive government in which a ruler has complete power.

vanishing point In drawing, the point in the distance at which parallel lines appear to meet in a perspective drawing.

vernacular The common, everyday language spoken by a population or group of people.

villa A large estate or residence located in the country or outside a town.

workshop A place where heavy work is carried out, a factory. In the Renaissance, an artist's workshop was run by a master artist who, with the help of various apprentices and assistants, produced works of art. The master artist directed the organization and production of his own workshop.

Index

Index